PARADOXICAL PHOENIX: IGNITE

PARADOXICAL PHOENIX: IGNITE

A Poetry Collection

By

Leslie Bertrand

Published by Paradoxical Phoenix Press
An imprint of Nighthawk Universal LLC
Charleston, South Carolina

ISBN 978-1-960270-00-9 (eBook)
ISBN 978-1-960270-01-6 (Paperback)

CONTENTS

III. SYSTEM

IV. LOST

V. FOUND

VI. ACCEPT

VII. FORGIVE

VIII. HEAL

FOREWORD

I've known Leslie since we were teenagers at neighboring high schools on the Connecticut shoreline in the early to mid-1980s. If you told us we'd jointly publish a collection of her poetry, but not until our late middle-age, I know what the reaction would have been. The scale of the years to come is meaningless at that age, but so much of what makes this venture possible had not yet even passed into existence: the Internet, the smart phone, social media, eBooks, print-on-demand books, etc.

Across all those years, though, Leslie has been writing. A lot.

Her social media followers are aware of how prolific she is. But the actual volume is as staggering as the high quality is consistent—more than you would ever find in forty-year-old notebooks of teenage ennui, angst and solace.

It was a necessary and rewarding challenge to title the many unnamed poems and organize them thematically. I feel it is unfinished, given how many belong in more than one section. But that may lead to a richer experience for the reader to decide where I'm wrong.

Leslie's adult career as an emergency and critical care nurse had pushed her empathic nature to the edge, but the precipice is where the best of this work is done. If there's any doubt, I hope her first collection will stand as proof.

Paul

BECOME

WHO'S THAT GIRL?

I'm that girl,
The one who skips on the beach
Dances in the rain
Sings in the shower
Howls at the moon
Gets lost in the woods,
Who prays by the fire.

I'm that girl,
The one who still hopes and dreams
Who has loved and lost
Who has crashed and burned
And risen from the ashes.

I'm that girl,
Who stopped talking and started doing
Who stopped settling
Who dared to believe in herself
Who lost all the filters,
and dared to expose her soul.

HAVING A BLAST

She dances uninhibited
To the music in her head
She stays out late
When she should be in bed

She really is quite shy
But she's not easily led
She feels like crying
But she laughs instead

She has fire and passion
She has rhythm and grace
She has a zest for living
That shows in her face

She's a loner and a gypsy
She is wild and free
She's living her life
The way she wants it to be

She won't be contained
She won't be caged
She will break all the rules
Of any game that you play

She is bold and confident
She has come into her own
No matter where she travels
She makes any place home

She's done regretting
The things in the past
She's taking a chance
And she's having a blast!

ACTRESS

I am a consummate actress
And no one can tell
That even though I'm smiling and laughing
I am still living in hell

I joke and I tease
For it helps hide the pain
When you feel like you keep losing
And you have nothing left to gain

I cry outside in the rain
So you don't see my tears
I scream into the void
Where no one can hear

I fade into the background
For I'm quite well aware
Of the perils and pitfalls
That await me out there

I prefer solitude and silence
To parties and events
Peace and quiet
Is my natural bent

You can't tell what I'm thinking
As I gaze into your eyes
When I tell you my thoughts
They always take you by surprise

I can change my appearance
On a whim or a dare
It's just a matter of rearranging
My clothes and my hair

You may not even notice me
As I slip on by
But that's OK
I never like to say goodbye.

DREAMING INTO THE REAL

I'm spreading my wings
I'm learning how to fly
It takes time to get lift
To soar high in the sky

Watch me now
I'm ready to go
It's time to begin
A whole new show

Watch me now
As I find my way
As I relearn how to laugh
Dance and play

Watch me sail
Navigating the breeze
I can adjust my sails
No matter how stormy the seas

Watch me, my dear
As I smile at you
And know that the strength of your love
Is making my dreams come true.

SOME DAYS

Some days I'm high
Some days I'm low
Some days I feel
I have a long way to go

Some days I laugh
Some days I cry
Some days I ponder
The reasons why

Why must we argue?
Why must we fight?
Why are there so many definitions
Of what's wrong and what's right?

Why can't we wake up
And realize it's time
Time to stand up, to do what's right
Time to make a choice, fight your own fight

If you want to see change
It's all up to you
No one else
Can do what you do

You make a difference
Each and every day
It's up to you to decide
The role that you'll play

Do you want to be thrust into the spotlight
On center stage?
Or is being a part of the chorus
What keeps you engaged?

Set your mind free
Break out of your box
Give something new a chance
You may discover it rocks

Some days I jump
To make that unknown leap
Some days I fail
And I land in a heap

But every day I wake up
And I keep giving it a try
Because at the end of the day
I am the reason I fly.

ALWAYS A DANCER

In my dreams
I'm dancing on stage
To ethereal music
That leaps off the page

I'm always a dancer
Tap, jazz or ballet
I've done it for ages
It's a part that I play

Lifetime after lifetime
I've moved to the beat
I'm unable to contain
The rhythm of my feet

The music entrances me
So I whirl and I dance
My heart is so full
I get lost in a trance

The notes they lift me
High above this plane
This beautiful music
Helps keep me sane

I hope you can discover
This ancient, wonderful art
Just get up and get moving
For that's where we all start.

TOUCHING THE DIVINE

I am the light in the darkness
The eye of the storm
The refuge you seek
When it's too much to be borne

I am the alpha and the omega
And everything in between
I am the end and the beginning
The seen and unseen

I am all that there is
All that ever will be
How then do you think
You can know all of Me?

You see but a glimpse
You've begun to believe
You can't truly grasp it all
It's too much to conceive

I am the infinite all knowing
I exist outside of time
You'll know when you touch me
For there's no other love like mine.

ZEBRA

All my life I've been a zebra
Nothing ever goes as it should
When you hear hoof beats you think horses
Logic says that you would

I'm a big fan of logic
It helps me to figure things out
But sometimes I find logic fails me
And then I begin to doubt

My life has always been different
The only drumbeat I dance to is mine
I can tell you it isn't easy
But I'm having one hell of a time

I don't know where I'm going
But I sure as hell know where I've been
I've walked this path many times before
Now I'm doing it all, again

I won't change my coat or my colors
I'm tired of trying to fit in
I've discovered my voice and my passion
Now let the fun begin!

THE WATER SINGS

The water sings to me
I hear it calling my soul
I climb into the river
Ready to go with the flow

At first the ride is gentle
It's soothing and smooth
But underneath the water
Obstacles are hidden from view

I navigate the currents
With caution and care
I don't want to get caught in the undertow
While I am unaware

I see the rapids ahead
There is nowhere else to turn
I have no choice but to continue forward
Paddling furiously while I learn

Every course has its challenges
Its twists and turns and rocks
I've become more adept at navigating them
They're no longer a shock

I love floating down this river
This universal stream they call life
I know I've passed this way before
More than once or twice

The water sings to me
It sings the song of my soul
I'll never tire of navigating it
For there are always new places to go.

THE ILLUMINATION

The music started
And I drifted away
I could see, hear and feel
Every note that was played

The notes vibrated
They hung in the air
The colors exploding in my mind
And then lingering there

Somehow though
I've become more aware
That's the thing
That I'm trying to share

Echoing endlessly
All through the night
The music grows louder
At dawns' first light

The illumination reveals
All of natures song
The moment invites you
To come sing along

So you hum and you drift
Suddenly you're floating in space
You're a little confused
As to how you got to this place

You're easily distracted
As the wonders unfold
You wander what's next
Because now you've grown bold

The journey is commencing
As you wander the path
Step by step at your own pace
For you know it leads home at last.

TIGER

I am a tiger
I have earned my stripes
They are the result
Of winning life's fights

I am a tiger
Here me roar
You may knock me down
But I'll come back for more

I am a tiger
I don't run, I chase
I will pursue my prey
At a relentless pace

I am a tiger
I hunt through the night
I am proud and I'm free
I won't give up that right

I am a tiger
You could be too
Listen to your inner voice
What is it saying to you?

SELF TALK

You see things
Other people don't
You take chances
Other people's won't

I see you smile
When you want to cry
I watch you go on living
When you want to roll over and die

You lost it all
And started again from scratch
Now I'm watching you
Get it all and more of it back

It's a risk you take
A path you choose
Every day YOU decide
Whether you win or lose

Two steps forward
One step back
Just keep on going
'Cause baby, you're back on track

I'm going to watch you fly
I've seen you earn your wings
Get ready my love,
Let's see what the future brings!

HERE'S TO YOU

Here's to the loners, the misfits
The outcasts and freaks
Those who've often felt the heat
Of their tears on their cheeks

Here's to the ones
Who don't fit in a box
Here's to the individuals
Who dodge all the rocks

Here's to the brave
The courageous and strong
You really are all right
They're the ones that are wrong

Here's to the soloist
Bravely singing her song
And to all those who decide
They DON'T want to follow along

Here's to the explorers
Who've gotten lost and then found
Here's too all of you
Boldly breaking new ground

Here's to the rebels
The squeaky wheels and the pests
Here's to those of you
Who don't follow the herd like the rest

Here's to all of us
Who are doing our own thing
Here's to loving
The freedom that brings!

A CHIP

You said you think
I have a chip on my shoulder
I'm here to tell you
You're lucky it isn't a boulder

You have no idea
The life that I've lived
I have no desire to explain
All I've had to give

You sit there in judgment
From high up on your hill
Toss back another drink
And count the money in your till

I wonder if you know
How far I've had to crawl
To regain my strength
To get back on my feet at all

You have no idea
Baby, you haven't got a clue
But I have to mention
It's not my job to enlighten you

You see face value
You don't look under the hood
You see the spit-shine and polish
And you call it all good

I've never been content with the surface
The treasure lies deeper within
But you'll never uncover it
It's not a prize that you win

I'm not your possession
I cannot be bought
I am a one of a kind treasure
That has been divinely wrought

So sit back and watch me
Stay back where it's safe
I'm going out to make it happen,
I'm not going to wait.

THE SONG

I hear the song of the universe
The siren call of the sea
The vibrations echo everywhere
I hear them calling me

It's a very subtle sensation
When you hear the call
You have to really pay attention
If you wish to hear it all

At first you may wonder
About that ringing in your ears
But lose yourself it the echoes
It's amazing what you will hear

It's all one big symphony
That reverberates in your heart
Once you learn to uncover it
You're off to a really good start

Sit a while in the silence
You'll begin to hear what it has to say
You'll begin to wonder
How you knew any other way

It's such a vast universe
This place that we call home
This is but one incarnation
So many other places we may roam

Don't discount your time here
On this third rock from our sun
You have so much left to do
Your work had just begun

So take a few more minutes
Before you start your day
To breathe in the song of the universe
Starting right here in our Milky Way.

I'M GONNA

You said I'm gonna burn my bridges
I asked for gasoline and a match
Because I'm gonna light a bonfire
And start all over from scratch

I'm gonna rise from the ashes
For phoenixes never burn
We only come back stronger
From the lessons we have learned

I'm gonna stoke the fire
I'm reborn in the flames
I'm gonna keep moving forward
To ensure that things will change

I'm gonna rise even higher
Who knows how high I'll soar
Every time I think the ride is over
It begins again once more

I'm gonna go the distance
I'm gonna persevere
I'm gonna make a difference
And I'm gonna begin right here.

THE VOICE

The voice, the voice
It calls me to dance
It dares me to go out
To take one more chance

The voice, the voice
That I hear in my head
You wouldn't believe
Some of the things that it's said

The voice, the voice
Whispers, listen to me
My rational brain says
Now how can this be?

The voice, the voice
Is it my own?
Or is some celestial intelligence
Ringing my phone?

The voice, the voice
The call of the muse
It's meant to be nurtured
Not used and abused

The voice, the voice
Has wisdom to share
It's just getting clearer
As I become more aware

The voice, the voice
Be it day or night
It calls to me
It compels me to write

The voice, the voice
Some days it's clear
Other days it's distant
And not easy to hear

The voice, the voice
Quiet the din
In the well of silence
You'll hear it within

The voice, the voice
As I drift off at night
Whispers, well done
Now become one with the light

The voice, the voice
I hear its song
The universe is singing
Won't you sing along?

LIGHT OF DAWN

I wander through the valleys
I wander through the hills
I wander by the still lake shore
The silence gives me chills

In the silence of the morning
By the dawn of the sun's first light
I hear the birds calling
And I watch them all take flight

The sun rises so slowly
It's giving a majestic show
It feels like it passes in moments
But the reveal is soft and slow

I stand in the shifting colors
In the tranquil light of dawn
I take this moment to gather all my strength
Knowing I must soldier on

So I take another look
And another cleansing breath
Knowing that as I go forward
I will always give my best.

CHILD

Child you are so radiant
You shine with your own inner light
You brighten every day
And illuminate my nights.

Child you are a wonder
So curious and small
I watch you reach out and grab the world
Then you try to taste it all.

Child you are so nimble
So gracious and so quick
You discover things at lightning speed
You're a flame devouring a wick.

Child you are learning
Each and every day
It is my utmost privilege
To help you along the way.

Child there are many lessons
So many things for you to know
I'm delighted to walk beside you
As you blossom and you grow.

Child I hope you never know
How I lie awake at night
How hard I hope and pray for you
That everything is all right.

Child you carry my hopes
My dreams and wishes too
For all those things I never had
I wish them all for you.

Child what I'm trying to say
And I hope you know it's true
I'm thankful you're in this life
And all my love remains forever with you.

FULL MOON INTENTION

May the words I whisper
Be what you need to hear
May they always be pleasant
To your ears

May all my words
Be straight and true
May I always speak
My heart to you

May you never mistake
My intent
May I always communicate
Just what I meant

May your heart be open
As well as your mind
May all your actions
Be forever kind

May your spirits soar
With the rising sun
May you sleep peacefully
When your day is done

May this prayer
Be carried upon the winds
May the Great Creator
Take it in

May the blessings
Overflow
For as above
So below.

BALANCE

I am a balance
Of darkness and light
I'm a child of the morning
And a queen of the night

The fire within
Burns hot and bright
I see my own shadow
And I dance with delight

My eyes are wide open
The universe is in sight
Drifting higher
And feeling alright.

LAST OF THE LIGHT

How far will you go
To follow your dreams?
Will you let them lead you
To places unseen?

Are you content
At the end of each day?
When the last of the light
Is fading away?

When your head hits the pillow
As you lay down each night
Do you fall asleep easily
And let your dreams take flight?

What would you do
If you had your choice?
What does your soul tell you?
What would make you rejoice?

Where you go
Is all up to you
If you have the courage
To see this thing through

Take a chance
To make a change
Or do nothing
And things remain the same.

DAMAGE

TASTING GRIEF

Broken hearts and shattered dreams
Taste like bitter ashes and curdled cream

When they are crushed beneath your feet
Your head hangs low in abject defeat

You know this old acquaintance, grief

The tears they well and fall from your eyes
You want to scream your anguish to the skies

Instead you reach a compromise
Slipping back into your old disguise

Stuffing it all down, deep inside

You thought you'd hold it all together
But nothing ever lasts forever

For even when the dance is done
Still the melody lingers on

The real work has only just begun

Close the door and lock it tight
Wide awake all through the night

Nothing seems to make it right
Not even fifty-fifty hindsight

The last thing I wish to do is fight

Feel the pain burn in my chest
Just need to take a deeper breath

Only emotions can make such a mess
Breathe some more and take a rest

You can take these final steps

Let yourself feel that pain
Let the tears fall down like rain

Despite their tracks they leave no stain
I stare unseeing through the window pane

Knowing it will never be the same.

BURNED LIKE LIQUID FLAME

The tears burned
Like liquid flame
I screamed and cried
As I said your name

There was no warning
You were taken away
It felt like time stopped
For me that day

You were here
Then you were gone
Now, it's just your memory
That lingers on

I miss your smile
I miss you laugh
I miss your face
But you won't be back

Somewhere, someday
We will meet again
I only wish
That I knew when.

NOT OK, TODAY

There's no way to go back
And believe the lies
I wish that I could
Believe me I've tried

I wish I could unsee
The things that I've seen
If you can't understand
You don't know what I mean

Some days I wish
I could un-ring that bell
Would things be better or worse?
Only time will tell

I wish I could forget
All the cries and the pain
Once you've heard them
You're never the same

I can still smell
The blood on the road
The smell of antifreeze
Puddled in the cold

I still wake up
Screaming at night
Sweating and shaking
As I reach for the light

I take a deep breath
As the echoes fade away
It will be OK, they said
Maybe, but not today.

HIDDEN

In the shadows secrets dwell
Of many things I would not tell
Pain I had to lock away
Just to make it through another day

Lost in darkness, seeking light
Tired of the endless fight
Draw the darkness all around
Hiding, hiding, make no sound

Take the pill and wash it down
Now it's quiet and I'm unwound
Stagger in to try to sleep
Lying there I just weep

Wishing for a different way
Dreading every single day
Falling deeper into that well
Trapped in my own personal hell

Sit and watch the new sun rise
Wipe the tears from my eyes
Realize that to make this change
Nothing can remain the same

Take the slate and wash it clean
Immerse myself in all things green
Discover nature peace and love
Watch the blessings fall from above

Before you think this tales untrue
I assure you I did make it through
For step by step it takes some time
To rediscover your lost peace of mind.

THE VISION FADED

The echoes from your screams
Shattered my peaceful dreams
Though many miles away
I heard them clear as day

In the middle of the night
I knew something wasn't right
The tears ran down my face like rain
All I could do was say your name

I felt you reach for me
I wasn't sure how this could be
But somehow through time and space
All I saw was your face

You smiled and said goodbye
You told me not to cry
You said it was okay
That we'd meet again someday

Then the vision faded
Yet my fear had not abated
For envisioning my life without you
Is not what I wish to do

We hadn't bargained on fate
Sadly, now, it is too late
For there never will be any sense
In losing life to violence.

A NURSE REFLECTS

Sad lonely child with tears on her face
Locked away, told you're such a disgrace
Struggles blindly to understand and to see
How exactly do these people love me?

Daily laden with abuse, guilt and shame
Her view of her world has forever been changed
Unable to find peace, not even inside
Seeking the shadows knowing there she can hide

Listening closely, observing, peeking out to see
Searching for an opening to finally be free
Totally feeling nothing, she is just numb
She cuts into her skin to see her blood run
Believing her dreams have ended before they've begun

This is the only release she can see
Lost, trapped, and buried emotionally
Thin, pale, wounded and weak
She hates herself more for the tears on her cheeks

The weight of those shed burden her down
She continues to struggle to try not to drown
Flailing and slashing she grasps about
Totally unexpected; the hand reaching out

Out of the darkness she emerges to see
A face leaning over; hey there, that's me!
I will take your hand when you want to hide
I wipe away all of the tears that you've cried
While you were lost I remained by your side.

CASUAL WORDS

You said you love me
I said, you tried
I said, I love you
My feelings you easily denied

You made me laugh
You also made me cry
You made me so confused
A part of me died inside

There was no safe way
For me to feel
No matter how I felt
You said, that's not real!

When I cried
Those words you said,
I'll give you something to cry about
Keep ringing in my head

Go ahead and laugh
But not too loud
It just wouldn't do
To attract a crowd

Don't be so sensitive
It's not that bad
Stop being upset
It's making me mad

You're such a problem
I cannot think
See what you do
You drive me to drink

This is the litany
Of my childhood years
This is where I acquired
All the shame and the fears

A child hears
All that you say
You may not believe it
But it never fades away

Watch the words
That you choose to share
Because those developing minds
Are fully aware

The damage that is inflicted
With your casual words
Are something that really,
Can never be unheard.

CONSTANT BLEEDING

Your disappointment is palpable,
a weight in the air

It's a bitter aftertaste in my mouth,
knowing that despite my best efforts
in your eyes I always fall short;
never quite attaining the perfection
that you seek to see
when you think of me

I'm tired
of trying to walk
on the razor's edge of your tongue

For you wield painful words
with the unerring accuracy
of an Olympic archer

I grow weak
from the constant bleeding loss
of wounds both new and old,
never allowed to heal.

MY MEMORIES

You would not believe
Some of the shit that I've seen
It's permeated my soul
And stained my dreams

No one ever told me,
I've heard those words said
Now those memories
Won't get out of my head

I've held onto hands
While families cried
Hanging on to the edge of the bed
Where their loved one has died

I've searched in rivers,
Oceans and lakes
I'm intimately familiar
With the lives that that takes

It only takes moments
To founder and drown
Sometimes a splash and a scream
Others, there isn't a sound

I've seen bullet holes and stab wounds
In bodies uncounted
I've seen it all for years
And the politicians do nothing about it

I've done rape kits on women and kids
I've talked them out of the places they've hid
I've watched an auger tear into a young mans' chest
I've held newborn babies to their mothers breasts

I've helped to birth the young
I've buried the old
A witness to it all
I've watched the stories unfold

Sometimes I lie awake
Through the darkest of nights
Seeing it all again
And remembering the fight

Other times I do sleep
And it's then that I dream
And I realize those memories
Cannot be unseen

But I don't want to forget
That doesn't seem right
For who else would remember them
And their incredible light?

NO OFF SWITCH

It feels like
My brain's on fire
The neurons keep firing
A million miles an hour

I can't seem to stop
The movie in my head
It's most intrusive
When I'm lying in bed

There's no off switch
That I can find
That stops those images
Deep in my mind

Before I know it
They've gotten me carried away
Right back to a place
I never meant to stay

All I want
Is to stop the race
And restore peace and quiet
Back to that place.

COMPLICATED CHARACTER

You can never take back
Those words that you said
Hurtful and hateful
They ring in my head

I'm not sure you realize
The power of the words you wield
In the ones you choose to speak
Your character is revealed

You think you are
So clever and wise
But now I see through
Your complicated disguise

Did you understand
When you rang that bell
That the reverberations would resonate
Straight into hell?

I'm sure you didn't
But, you see time always tells
All I can do now
Is stand back and wish you well.

DIAGNOSIS

A small part of me
Died inside
When I gave you the news
And saw the fear in your eyes

I've seen that look
So many times before
It never gets easier
It's a look I abhor

I know that you feel
Hopeless and lost
I know that you're laying there
Adding up the cost

In dollars and cents
In suffering and pain
Am I watching my life
Go right down the drain?

The future is uncertain
In a moment it's changed
In just a few minutes
You're life's completely rearranged

I sat there beside you
While you cried
While you struggled to process facts
That could not be denied

No matter where
This path shall lead
Know I'm there beside you
As long as you need.

THE CHILD DIED

Hope has died
With the absence of the child's cries

In the silence,
not denied

Confirmation,
it was not a lie

Standing here
by your side

Wracked by the grief,
you shake and sigh

Crying out to God,
Just tell me why

A silent witness,
as inside my mind,

I keep repeating,
God knows we tried.

CHOKING ON DARKNESS

Lost and found then lost again
Feel the darkness as it descends
Trapped in this prison within my mind
The thoughts that dwell here are most unkind

Despair feels like a heavy cloak
I cannot breathe; I just choke
Searching for bits and pieces of me
Floundering, I am lost at sea

Staring for hours off into space
Feel the tears trace down my face
So dark and deep this well of pain
Crying, sobbing, my tears fall like rain

They say that it will be All Right
Still I lie awake at night
Knowing it's a daily fight
Seeking that elusive light

Tired now I wish to yield
To walk right off this playing field
But, if I lay down instead of walk away
Would the game continue anyway?

YOU WONDER

You're chasing a high
You can't hope to obtain

All you're reaching for
Is an end to the pain

You keep going back
It's an endless refrain

You struggle on in this world
While slowly going insane

You're watching your life
Wash right down the drain

Wondering with all this loss
Where is the commensurate gain

You view the world
With increasing disdain

You're beginning to learn
That it's all just a game

You've trying to let go
Of guilt, blame and shame

Daily you wonder
Why you came

For while everything changes
It somehow remains the same.

SYSTEM

THIS PILL

Just shut up
And take your pill
We have a new one for you
Here is your prescription to fill

Here's a white pill
It will make you smile
Now take this blue one
And you'll sleep for awhile

There's a pill to lift you up
One to slow you down
We have plenty of pills
To go around

Why make a change
When you can just pop a pill
When did we start believing
They'd cure all our ills?

Take this pill
Don't you dare think
Wash that down
With this big cold drink

Is it any wonder
That we're so confused
When we try to treat ourselves
With pills and booze?

FOR THE CHILDREN

I weep for the children
The ones who don't know
How to swim in the ocean
Or sled in the snow

I weep for the children
The ones who can't shout
The ones stuck inside
Who just can't get out

I weep for the children
Now masked and muzzled
How soon will it be
Before they're totally off track

I weep for the children
Who can no longer engage
The ones who don't know what to do
With their anger and rage

I weep for the children
Who are made to confirm
Will a generation of mindless drones
Become our new norm?

I weep for the children
Those lost in the upheaval
We're headed for times
That are appearing medieval

I weep for the children
And all that we've lost
You should weep for the children
Who pay the ultimate cost.

IS IT ANY WONDER

Don't believe what you see
Believe what you hear
We are trying to subjugate you
You must live in fear

You must follow the messages
That you are given
We want you hungry
Desperate and driven

We want you to struggle
We want you to fight
We want you cowed
Afraid of doing what's right

We want your money
We want your power
We want it all
In our untouchable tower

Don't ask questions
Don't hesitate
You must act right now
Before it's too late

You must have this thing
Look it's on sale
Pay no attention
That you're set up to fail

You must acquire
You must make do
You must succeed
You know this is true

So many messages
Assaulting our ears
Is it any wonder
You're living in fear?

THE NEW NORMAL

Hey, little child
Hidden inside
I see you there
With your eyes open wide

What do you witness?
What do you see?
What are you thinking,
When you're looking at me?

I smile and nod
You give a laugh
Ah, that precious joy on your face
How I pray that it lasts

You can't see our smiles
Hidden under our masks
But we can feel that connection
And that's all I can ask.

WHAT THE HELL

I look around me
And wonder, what the hell?
What the hell happened to this world
I used to know so well?

What the hell happened?
It wasn't overnight
When the hell did things
Stop going right?

What the hell
Do we keep fighting for?
Haven't you had enough
Of death and war?

What the hell
Can our leaders be thinking?
Or maybe they aren't
And they've just taking up drinking

What the hell is happening
With this inflation?
Are they truly trying
To cripple us as nation?

What the hell am I witnessing?
When will it end?
How the hell can we change
This downward trend?

How the hell can we not ask these questions
Is what I want to know
How the hell can you sit by
And just watch this shit show?

RIGGED GAME

The shit, I feel
Has hit the fan
And we're all tap dancing
As fast as we can

The game is fixed
The rig is in
You're going to lose
For there's no way to win

Masterfully woven
This dastardly plot
You can't remember
Because you already forgot

Bit by bit
The aim is to take it all
Most won't even notice
Until they fall

Roll up your pants
You can't save your shoes
The bullshit's rising fast
Just watch the news

It's an endless litany
Of hate and fear
More and more
That's becoming clear

You'll own nothing
And you'll be happy
Well how come losing it all
Makes me feel so crappy?

LIARS CONSPIRE

Do you feel like the weight of the world
Is dragging you down
Like you want to smile
But you can only frown?

Do you feel dragged out
Tired and spent
Like you knew where you were going
But then forgot where you went?

Do you feel like things
Are turned inside out
Like everything's changed
But you don't know how it came about?

Do you feel a little lost
Dazed and confused
Consumed by the bullshit
That you see on the news?

Do you feel like it's all
Just one big game
Where there are no winners
Only losers in a world gone insane?

Do you feel like it's a collection
Of illusions and lies
That the posturing is empty
And they'll never compromise?

Huh,
I'm not surprised.

NO ESCAPE

In your own personal hell there's no easy escape
For it's a prison you've built from your own mistakes
You huddle within and look up at the sky
You find yourself wondering, "oh good God why?"

You know it hasn't always been suffering and pain
Still you see your life washing right down the drain
You feel like you're drowning and going insane
You keeping wishing for sunlight but you're stuck in the rain

Some days you sit there and wonder
Would it be easier now, just to go under?
So you try really hard to go with the flow
Then you wonder just how deep it can go?

Some people wish for fortune and fame
You'd be content for a day without pain
You're feeling lost and really alone
You have no idea how the hell to get home

You're tired of hearing folks say, it's all right
When you wish you knew where you were sleeping tonight
You're not sure where you will go anymore
You've been turned away from so many doors

It's not easy to be down and out
To see everyone else rushing about
It looks like they all have somewhere to go
It makes you feel even emptier you know

Lost in the bustle of making their way
No one notices at the end of the day
That instead of climbing into a comfy warm bed
You're out there sleeping on the sidewalk instead

And when you catch the attention of passers by
Not one of them is able to look you in the eye
At best they might toss you some money
Shake their heads and mutter, "sorry honey"

This has become a matter of course
As sad situation of human discourse
But if we don't continue to spread the word
These voices will never really be heard

It's time to question our societal norm
There's a need for some major reform
It's amazing what we've learned to tolerate
Let's make a change before it's too late.

PULL THAT WOOL

I live in a world
Where up's become down
Where somehow everything
Has gotten turned around

They'll have you believing
That day's become night
They want to convince you
The wrong thing is right

They want you to surrender
Your hopes and your dreams
They bleed you dry
As they feed on your screams

They want you to believe
That when it's all said and done
They're doing the best thing
For everyone

They don't want you to think
Or even to question
It's all going to hell
But don't you dare mention

Don't you dare look
Don't check your own facts
Sit back and take a video
Don't bother to act

Believe what they tell you
On the mainstream news
Don't you dare disseminate
A new point of view

Just you keep quiet
Silently go down with your ship
We'll give you a push
To send you off on your trip

The man pulling your strings
Is hidden deep inside
Isn't it time to pull
The wool from your eyes.

CONFORM

Conform, conform
Fit in with the norm

Want a new point of view
We'll give it to you

Erase those thoughts in your head
We'll give you new ones instead

You think you know up from down
Wait, we'll turn you around

Focus on the horrors you see
Not the underlying humanity

Just tune in to the news
For more daily abuse

Have I failed to mention
Don't think to question

Do you really think you are free
With your blind loyalty?

THEY WANT

They want you to believe
The world isn't safe any more
They want you to stay inside
Behind your locked doors

They want you to forget
Your hopes and your dreams
They're drowning them out
In discordant screams

They want you to believe what you hear
Not what you see
They want to continue
To divide you and me

They want you to be fearful
To be angry and scared
They want you submissive
And kept unaware

They want you distracted
Lost and alone
They want you subjugated
Not to leave home

They want to spoon feed their messages
And have you swallow them whole
They don't want you to see the price you're paying
And how it's taking its toll

They want you ignorant
Until it's too late
Until all you can do
Is blindly accept that it's fate

They want you to believe
That you'll be happy with less
They're trying to tell you
Things aren't one hell of a mess

They want you subdued
And not doubting of their plan
So will you begin to ask questions now
Or wait until it's all out of your hands?

YOU THINK YOU KNOW

The tired man stood begging
On the side of the road
He was shivering and shaking
Out there in the cold

You could tell by looking
He had no where to go
His steps were measured
Patient and slow

His backpack beside him
Neatly at his feet
His sign said
Hungry, I'm just looking to eat

The look on his face
Communicated his defeat
I'd seen him yesterday
Today was a repeat

No one stopped
To give him a cent
For in their minds they already knew
How that money would be spent

He'd just use it
For drugs and drink
It doesn't matter what they say
I know how they think

No one knew
The road he'd taken
They all had their assumptions
But they were all mistaken

It wasn't gambling
Drugs or drink
He'd just gotten sick
And it took them over the brink

He never thought
His family would live in a tent
But that was all they could afford
So that's where he went

He never thought
He would begin to despair
Until he learned
That nobody cared.

WHAT IS HIDDEN

Raise that false flag
Higher up into the air
Wave it around and draw attention
So everyone knows it is there

Create a simple distraction
Do you remember ring and run?
The game's afoot, the stakes are higher
And now no one is having fun

Pay no attention to what is hidden
We'll reveal what you need to see
Don't think to ask a question
That just the way things are going to be

The noose is slowly tightening
Nothing escapes its grasp
Like slowly turning up the temperature
You hardly notice until you begin to gasp

Everyone is drowning
No one cares to throw a rope
Is it really any wonder then
Why people are struggling to cope?

ALL ANGRY, ALL THE TIME

Everyone is angry
Everyone is pissed
I look around and wonder
What the hell I missed

Angry in the checkout
Angry in the car
People are really fucking angry
No matter where they are

Road rage on the freeway
Shootings in the mall
Is it any wonder
I choose to go out at all?

Don't you call me Karen!
Don't you tell me to wait!
I just told you to jump
Why do you hesitate?

It's all instant gratification
No one can stand a delay
They want it right this second
No matter the price you pay

Anger in the headlines
Anger in your home
I'm beginning to wonder
If anger is all we know.

WHY ANGELS WEEP

I inquired of the angel
Why do you weep?
He replied, I never thought I'd see humans
End up as sheep

Blindly following
No matter who doth lead
It's such a tangled thread
Woven into humanities weave

What ever happened
To "in God we trust"?
When did we start believing
The government would take care of us

When did it all
Become so veiled and cloaked
When did people begin
To lose their collective hope?

BIG PHARMA BLUES

Take these pills
This is what they said
They will stop the images
Playing out in your head

Take these pills
These will stop the pain
They don't tell you
You'll slowly go insane

Take these pills
They will help your depression
In fact you won't feel much of anything
That you'll feel like confessing

Take these pills
They'll make the anxiety go away
What does it matter
If you sleep all day

Take these pills
They'll make you thin
Pay no attention to your heart
While it's racing within

Take these pills
They'll help keep you awake
You'll be wound up like a top
You'll shiver and you'll shake

Take these pills
One after the other
You ignore treating the underlying cause
You won't even bother

Take these pills
But consider the price you pay
Are you really improving your life
Or watching it all waste away?

NO END IN SIGHT

I'm living paycheck to paycheck
With no end in sight
Sometimes that uncertainty
Keeps me up all night

I'm not even working for peanuts
It's so little pay
Forget perks and benefits
They took those away

You pay a fortune for insurance
It's such a scam
They deny all your claims
And they don't give a damn

If you have a preexisting condition
You can still get insured
Kiss your money goodbye though
Because the cost is absurd

My cash flow is static
While the prices all rise
An endless cycle of greed
For which there is no disguise

You better breast feed your baby
If you want them to eat
Enfamil and Similac
Are now what's hot on the street

In many places you're prohibited
From collecting your own rain water
I feel like the people are sheep
Being fattened up for slaughter

They say we will have nothing
Sure looks like that game has begun
Sadly, I think we're all gonna lose
When it's all said and done.

THE CHORUS

I'm not going to drink your Kool-Aid
I'm not going to take your pills
I'm not going to line up for your injection
I'm tired of the lies that you spill

I'm tired of the deception
I'm tired of all of the lies
I think you count on our compliance
And us never getting wise

Things are becoming transparent
The veil is starting to thin
Now is the time to dig deep
Now you must look within

Nothing has been easy
Most of it's come with a fight
But don't you ever give up
Doing what you know is right

They're trying to silence the voices
Isn't that just a shame
Or course they don't want to hear it
When you are crying out for change

Isn't it time to stand up
To let your voice be heard
Now is not the time to remain silent
It's your job to spread the word

Why don't you join in the chorus
Why don't you speak this time
For right now the world is changing
Right now you can impact the design

What is it that you see
As you help to recreate this new earth?
Do you wish for something different?
What is that change worth?

JUST BUSINESS

It's just business
That's what they said
When they don't pay enough
To keep a roof over your head

It's just business
Is what we were told
You're certainly not worth
Your weight in gold

It's just business
It's a constant refrain
Over and over
It's etched into my brain

It's just business
You'll work all night
You'll do what we tell you
To get paid alright

It's just business
The employees come and they go
We'll post your position
Before your obituary, you know

It's just business
We're all here to make money
The fact that the underlings want too
Now that's downright funny

It's just business
Seems to me something is wrong
If you work 40 hours
You should be able to get along

It's just business
Don't you dare to get sick
Even with your Insurance
Your money goes quick

It's just business
As we're drowning in inflation
I think that the business of business
Is helping to kill this nation.

LOST

CONDITIONAL

You made your love conditional
A contractual obligation
Only it's always been one sided
Never an open ended negotiation

I still find it odd
You don't understand my hesitation
When everything I say and do
Is met with degradation

You wonder why I've withdrawn
I call it a tactical retreat
Over the years I've leaned to distance myself
It's not been an easy feat

Every present was a promise
Of emotional manipulation
A continual reminder
Of that unending insinuation

Nothing was ever offered
Without a calculated cost
By the time I figured that out
My sense of self was lost

I finally had to cut the cords
That were disguised so prettily in a bow
A complete excision was necessary
For me to finally let you go

It certainly isn't easy
I'm old for a brand new start
But it has been so worth it;
Rediscovering my heart.

RESIDUAL

I don't miss you
Not any more
Not since that day
That I closed the door

Always before
You dragged me back in
No matter how hard I tried
I just couldn't win

The difference now
Is that I've finally learned
Well, at least as far
As you are concerned

I'm still struggling
With some anger and pain
But it's that residual emotion
That's allowed me to change

I want to move forward
I'm tired of glancing back
Trying to anticipate
The next attack

So even though it's hard
To simply say, good bye
I'm done with regret
For now it's my time to fly.

WHAT YOU SAID

You say that you love me
But you don't want to try
You say you value my laughter
But it means more when I cry

You say you miss me
Then you don't call
You say you need to think
Then you say nothing at all

You say you're not ready
But you said I'm all in
You say I'll start over
But you never begin

You say that you're sorry
But your actions don't change
You say things will be different
But you don't turn the page

You say it's not over
But it never really began
You say let's work it out
But I don't think we can.

PRETTY WORDS

You were a fair weather friend
Not a long term lover
Believe me when I tell you my dear
There's a huge difference between one and the other

It was always about you and this moment
About the games you could play
You had no real intention
Of ever wanting to stay

You said, you don't know what to do with me
I said, what is there to do
And I knew right from that moment
That you'd never see things through

Still I wanted to believe
In all those pretty words you said
They were so seductive
When you whispered them in our bed

They never matched your actions
And I continued to ignore
All the opposite reactions
Until you walked right out the door

Now you've found someone else
You say she's the one for you
Will you sell her the same tired lies
Or will you finally try for truth?

I know that introspection
Isn't your strongest thing
You'd rather forget all about it
And just take another drink

Now I'll run into you upon occasion
Not as a lover or even a friend
Just someone whom I used to know
And I'll walk on by again.

KNOW HOW

I know how she feels
When she says I'm losing you
I know how she feels
When she realizes that it's true

I know how she feels
When you say you can't stay
I know how she feels
To watch you walk away

I know how she feels
Laying awake all night
I know she is wondering
If there's a way to make it right

I know how she feels
To feel lost and alone
Because I know how I felt
When you didn't come home.

FRESH GRIEF

I miss you every minute
Every hour of every day
My world is not the same
Since you went away

You left some big holes
That feel like they'll never be filled
I can't imagine anyone else
Able to foot the bill

I feel so lost and lonely
My days are quieter now
They tell me I have to go on living,
I'm struggling to remember how

You were there beside me
For oh so many years
You helped me to navigate
So many hopes and fears

It all passed by so quickly
In just the blink of an eye
Now I'm lost in my memories
And all I can do is cry.

IN THIS DANCE

You wonder why I'm angry
You say that I seem pissed
Baby I have to tell you
There's a few things that you missed

You tell me you'll do one thing
Then you turn and do another
You throw up so much bullshit
I have to duck and cover

Your lies are insidious
For you believe what you say
I wish you were more transparent
It'd be easier that way

I'm tired of this tango
It is chaotic passion and grace
It really is quite draining
Keeping up such a furious pace

I've bowed out of this encore
My time in this dance is through
It's much more peaceful on the sidelines
Rather than turning around in circles with you.

CHASE BACK THE DARK

I sat here and watched you
Walk right out the door
But I'm here to tell you
I don't burn for you, not anymore

I remember all of the words
All those things that you said
It's a kaleidoscope of memories
Tumbling around in my head

The sparks from our meeting
We soon fanned into flame
We jumped into that fire
In spite of the pain

Drawn to the magic
Contained in that spark
We hit the ground running
Hoping to chase back the dark

Too bad we were blinded
We just couldn't see
The impact it would have
On you and on me

Backwards and forwards
My love we did chase
Our emotions ran us about
All over the place

But one thing I've learned
Through the passage of time
Is that you just aren't ready
To call me mine.

I MISS

I miss your smile
I miss your laugh
God I miss you
I want it all back

I miss the talks
I miss the jokes
I miss you so much
It makes me choke

I miss the light
Shining in your eyes
I just miss us
And it makes me cry

I miss the ups
I even miss the downs
But what I miss the most
Is that you're not around.

BITS AND PIECES

I gave you bits and pieces of my heart
It began way back, right from the start
I never did imagine that you would walk away
And I would lose those pieces of myself someday

I gave you love and hope and faith
I gave and gave and you were happy to take
You kept saying, "things are fine"
I wish that I could turn back time

I'm not sure exactly when things went wrong
That moment when we no longer got along
I just knew that things weren't right
And I'd lie awake all through the night

Now I'm lying here all alone
Hoping and praying that you will phone
I'm trying to fill the holes you left
And I find that I am left bereft

For the only thing to fill them is you
Sadly I know that time is through
So I'll put back the pieces one by one
I'll be grateful when my task is done

Someday that ache will go away
I just have to take it day by day
Bits and pieces of my heart and mind
I will reclaim them all, given enough time.

WHAT LOVE IS

You said that you loved me
But you didn't, you know
For love isn't static
It changes and grows

It bends and it stretches
It can be worn thin and fine
Yet that thread will never break
Between two hearts, entwined

Love doesn't give up
It doesn't run away
It's always there
It isn't swayed

Love doesn't judge
It doesn't shame or blame
Love isn't fleeting
It isn't a game

Love is steadfast
It's courageous and bold
It's the glue that binds us together
Truth to be told

Those are some of the things
That love means to me
If they were the same to you
How different things would be.

CRACKED OPEN WIDE

All you could see
Was the smile outside
When inside she was screaming
And silently, she cried

Her heart had been broken
Cracked open wide
No matter where she ran
There was no place to hide

All she wanted to do;
Escape the pain of love denied
But she couldn't forget
No matter how hard she tried.

DID IT ANYWAY

I sat and cried
All alone
In my hand
I clutched my phone

One last time
A message from you
And those last words
Pierced me through

I don't know how
You could throw me away
But you went ahead
And did it anyway

You said you found
Someone new
You said she mattered
More to you

I could only sit
And watch you leave
Then close my door
To begin to grieve

It doesn't matter
Why you're gone
Only that the loss
Feels too much to be born

They say that time
It heals all wounds
But I'd rather have it
All renewed

So I hide away
My tears and pain
Until I'm ready
To face the world again.

FROM MY PAST

I got a message
From my past today
I thought I was seeing things
But it didn't go away

I stared in amazement
At the words upon my phone
I dropped my head into my hands
And let out a little groan

My gut tightened
I began to sweat
What the hell, I told myself,
Aren't you over this yet?

I took a deep breath
Then I took another
I knew if I didn't answer
I'd just lie awake and wonder

I don't know where this is going
But I sure know where it's been
The question that I ask myself
Are you going to do this, again?

BE AT PEACE

Excuse me, but have I failed to mention
How I used to long for your attention?
Just a few words from you
Were enough to warm me through

Try as I might
I'd dream of you all night
Thoughts of you filled my days
I was obsessed, I was half crazed

I'm not exactly sure why you captivated me
But I knew it was time to set myself free
I just had to learn to surrender
Despite the anxiety this engendered

Such a relief to let you go
Finally able to go with the flow
Personal freedom I have finally found
In learning how to become unbound

Now that I'm no longer stuck in my head
My days are never filled with dread
For moment by moment I can finally be
At peace in this sea of uncertainty.

FOUND

THE UNBURDENING

There are so many secrets
I whispered to you in the dark
Where in the anonymity of darkness
I can unburden my heart

It's easier to share
When I don't have to look into your eyes
For I just couldn't bear to look
And see your shock and surprise

It's isn't easy
It's surely not fair
To feel like I'm burdening you
With the pain hidden there

Imagine my shock
And my utter surprise
When not only did you thank me
But you wiped the tears from my eyes

You gathered me close
And you held me so tight
As you whispered,
Close your eyes, I've got you tonight.

INSTRUMENT

I love to lay back, close my eyes
and imagine you here
When I do that I swear
I can feel you draw near

I can feel the touch
of your lips on my skin
I relish in the sensation
and I drink it all in

My body is an instrument
and it's tuned to your touch
And with a sweep of your hand
you make me want you so much

It's a small bit of torture
to lie here alone
When I'm lonely and missing you
and wishing you were home

Just the idea
of being held in your arms
Feels like I am enclosed
in some magic charm

Know that I'll find you
as I drift off to sleep
For a small piece of my soul
that you keep

And when I awake
in the bright light of dawn
I'll weep just a little
upon seeing that you're gone.

WHAT I WANT

I want to snuggle up against you
Here in the dark
And listen to nothing
But the quiet beat of your heart

I want to lie next to you
With the lights turned down low
Knowing we have all night to explore each other
And no where else to go

I want to intoxicate myself
As I drink from your lips
Big, thirsty gulps
And the most delicate of sips

I want to smell the scent of you
As it perfumes the air
As it clings to your skin
Your clothes and your hair

I want to luxuriate
In every moment with you
And if I had the chance
That's just what I'd do.

DREAM A LITTLE DREAM

When I dream a little dream
I always dream of you
Of the way you make me laugh
With all the crazy things you do.

When I sit to sing a song
I wish to sing with you
A lovely little duet
Written just for two

When I walk through forests and fields
I think of us hand in hand
Whiling away the hours
No need for making plans

When I swim in the ocean deep
I think of you by my side
For when you're right there next to me
It doesn't seem so vast and wide

When I go to bed at night
I long to hold you in my arms
For when you're there beside me
I know I'm safe from harm

When I pray to God at night
I always pray for you
That His love will shine upon you
And everything you do

When I close my eyes
There's a smile upon my face
Knowing that when I see you
I'll drown in your embrace

When I'm grateful
For all that we get to share
I live in the present moment
By simply becoming more aware

So when I dream my little dream
I smile as I dream of you
Because in all of my realities
Your love comes shining through.

RIVER OF TIME

I want to sail with you
Along the river of time
To witness it all unfold
With your hand in mine

I want to stand beside you
As we weather each storm
When the chaos of each day
Feels it's too much to be borne

I want to walk with you
Among mountains and streams
Over beaches and fields
As we discover our dreams

I want to lay down beside you
At the end of each day
And let the warmth of your arms
Melt all my cares away

I want to wake up beside you
In every mornings first light
For each time that I see you
I know that things are just right.

THAT DANCE

It all began with a glance
Why not take that chance?
It was the last dance
A fortuitous circumstance

Your eyes met mine
We seemed to stop time
I was so aware
Of your considering stare

You walked across the floor
As the band readied once more
You took hold of my hand
And then took command

I danced in your arms
Not immune to your charms
Before that dance was through
I just wanted you

So back out onto the floor
A passionate encore
Knowing that night
We'd gotten it right

My partner, my friend
I've found you again
And such joy in this dance
This eternal romance.

IN THE WONDER

In that space between heartbeats
That transcends time
I can feel your aura
Blend into mine

I can feel
The weight of your soul
I see the fire in your eyes
And it makes me grow bold

I want to explore
All of the unknown with you
I don't want to stop
For we'll never be through

I want to feel your body
The silk of your skin
I want to hear the sound of your sighs
And drink it all in

I want us to get lost
To lose ourselves in one another
To embrace the magic
And rejoice in the wonder

I can imagine
The peace and the bliss
Because when we come together
There's nothing else like this.

WHAT I WANT II

I want to wander with you
Amidst the trees
To feel my hair
Get caught in the breeze

I want to watch the branches
As they sway and swing
And listen to the wind in the leaves
As it makes them sing

I want to stand upon the roots
Sunk deep in the ground
To listen to the hum of the forest
And its myriad sounds

I want to lie on a blanket
Gazing up at the stars
Simply holding your hand
As we lose track of the hours

I want to finish what we started
Because we never had the chance
It's hard to believe
And it's not about romance

I want that connection
I feel deep in my soul
Because when we're together
That's when I feel whole.

ELUSIVE MOMENTS

Whirl me around the dance floor
once more my love
for I have so enjoyed these dances with you

We began less skilled
but not beginners surely
for there have been other partners
but not experts
no, far from experts my dear
but I've always been eager to learn new things
and you've enjoyed yourself
for the most part
nothing is without effort

You've taken this challenge to heart
and finally stopped running
having surrendered
capitulated
and bowed to fate and
to a love more encompassing than we have ever known
and it's heaven

But
oh my love
it is hell as well
those moments of hurt confusion and separation
they are so painful
and those moments we embrace together
transcend the effort and struggle
and there in those elusive moments between heartbeats
we finally come home.

POST WAR LOVE

My darling, my love
We met at the fair
You were so young then
You laughed. I stared.

My sweetheart, my darling
You moved on to State
You had such ambitions
You studied quite late.

I waited at home while you learned a new way
So happy to see you
At the end of the day
Knowing and believing in our journey, underway.

My partner through time
We worked and we saved
Over the years
Our children we raised.

We watched as they struggled
As they learned and they grew
We supported and encouraged each other
To see this work through.

My beloved now we sit here on the porch
Watch the sun set in glory
Knowing the children
Have all gone forth.

I sit and I gaze at the lines on your face
I know each one
And they lend you such grace

Each line that is etched there
It tells of the tale
Of our life journey together
And all it entailed.

My beloved I will always
Carry you in my heart
I have from the beginning
And I will until we part.

I start the day knowing
The warmth of your touch
Now more than ever
Nothing means quite as much.

My darling, my love
You are still so fair
There is such joy in your laughter
Despite the gray in your hair.

Please know that I've always held you
Inside my heart
And as the day is ending
Even though we must part

That part of your soul
That you've gifted to me
Always connects us
Eternally.

THAT'S A FACT

If I say black
You say white
When it all goes wrong
You say, well that's all right

You just give in
I won't without a fight
You enjoy the darkness
I like the early morning light

I can't stop
And you won't go
You say yes
When I say no

I say I'm twisted
You think I'm broken
I like the written word
You prefer it spoken

You like the spotlight
I like to hide
I wear my heart on my sleeve
You keep yours deep inside

You like to go last
While I jump in first
I say things are getting better
You say they're worse

They say that opposites
Do indeed attract
I can tell you
For me that's a fact!

BELOVED

I hope that you can clearly see
Just how dear you are to me

In the morning with each sunrise
I see the love light shining in your eyes

I'm wrapped up in your warm embrace
As your smile illuminates your face

The joy and love you have within
Is like a beacon that draws me in

I know that what I feel is true
Because my love, I just ask you

So rarely though I need say
For I'm embraced by your love every day

So my darling I'd still like to say to you
I see you love, and you're shining too.

FLY WITH ME

Come my love
Fly with me
Remember what it is
To be wild and free

To roam beneath
The stars and moon
To bask in the warmth
Of the sun at noon

So many treasures
We have yet to uncover
As we simply learn
To enjoy one another

Who knows how high
We may soar
Myriad things
Still left to explore

One thing I've discovered
That does hold true
This journey is so precious
Shared with you.

JOURNEY

This connection that we both share
Crept up upon us most unaware

In a flash I saw your light
Like a beacon shining bright

I called to you, you answered me
Suddenly we both did see

That link that binds us two to one
Twin Flame Journey now begun

Back and forth, run and chase
Our emotions were all over the place

Soaring highs but crashing lows
We still had so far to go...

Initially meeting in the mind
As time went on we did find

This mirrored image that we share
Now we can find each other anywhere

I'm so blessed that I have found
You here with me this time around

We went ahead and took that chance
Now my love; how we dance!

As we continue to master this song
With all the others who've joined along

Here's to changing this paradigm
Because my love, now it's time!

IF I, WOULD YOU

If I become lost in the dark
And can't find my way
Would you hold my hand
Until the bright light of day?

If I wake up frightened
In the middle of the night
Would you hold me close
Until the fear loses its bite?

If you find me wandering
Confused and alone
Would you leave me to flounder
Or help guide me home?

If you witness me crying
Grieved and bereft
Would you sit and remind me
Of all I have left?

If you see my dancing
At the break of dawn
Would you come dance with me
Or simply walk on?

If I sing to you the song
Of the moon and the stars
Would you lose yourself in the tale
Or just think I'm bizarre?

I wonder if I reveal to you
All of my truths
Will you believe me
Or think I have a screw loose?

I LOVE

I love you on your good days
I love you when you're down
I love you when you're with me
And when you're not around

I love you when you laugh
I love you when you cry
I love you unconditionally
I can't quite explain why

I love you when you're happy
I love you when you're sad
I love you when you act crazy
I love you when you're mad

I love the silly songs you sing
I love the way you hold my hand
I love the way you look at me
When you're trying to understand

I love that you don't give up
I love that you persevere
I love that you're doing all of that
Next to me right here

I love to wake up to your smile
I love to fall asleep in your arms
I love how you make my day brighter
And how you keep me safe from harm

I love that we're still loving
Even after all these years
That we've somehow managed to overcome
All the doubts and fears

I love knowing my days
All include you
God willing I'll be able to keep loving you
All the rest of them too.

MINE

He watched in amazement
as she skipped to the shore
He had no idea
what he was in for

She flew over the sand
and played in the wind
He opened his heart
and then let her in

They cavorted and played
under the light of the moon
Neither one knew
this would end soon

He was surprised at the love
that shone in her eyes
She was shocked
at all of times that he cried

Despite the differences
they were happy, for a time
Until the tensions
started to rise

They kept all their worries
locked up inside
Anxious and stressful,
they got caught in the tide

So much easier
to push it all away
Rather than expose the hurts
to the harsh light of day

Locked into silence
there isn't much sound
Wondering,
where is that joy we had found?

Too easy it is
to get lost in the void
When your true feelings
trapped inside you avoid

So perhaps
a word of caution here
Never hesitate to tell them,
"you are so dear"

Open your mind
along with your heart
Communicate with your partner
it's a great start

We can drown in a sea
of what wasn't said
It tears at our heart,
the misunderstanding instead

If you want to remain together,
it's true
Love for me
has to equal love for you

Take the time
to show them and say
I love you more
every day

I give you this gift
of my mind and my heart
I know it's not much
but it is a start

I want you to know
I'll always be
Standing next to you,
eternally

I am never happier
then that movement in time
When you hold me tight and call me,
Mine.

ACCEPT

EMBRACE

Many times I've watched before
Seeing others pass through the hidden door
But I was on the outside looking in
Always unheard amidst the din

Why did others hold the key?
How could they have the answer, not me?
Many years I searched around
Feeling lost until I finally found

A path that made sense to me
Which I followed to set me free
Now I don't know why I did hesitate
To stride upon it in the first place

So many things I've come to find
Are so much easier in this frame of mind
If you are wondering, how?
The answer is; live in the now

Face what does come to pass
Work through the feelings and let them pass
Leave the past far behind
Present moment awareness you must find

Once you can learn to be
In the moment gratefully
It opens up that door
And with open heart you will soar

Through the barriers as you learn to fly
Happiness is the reason why
Learn contentment within your self
Put resentment on a shelf

Embrace a loving kinder way
Walk that path every day
You truly have no limits now
So spread your wings and find out how?

Maintain your life with love and light
Seeing how it sets things right
The more that can get to come this way
The easier it will get every day

It's time to change the paradigm
Time to embrace the love inside
I hope that you do hear this plea
And decide to come along with me.

KEEP ON SCROLLING

I never understood the point
Of living and telling a lie
Of saying things are OK
When you're merely scraping by

Someone asks you How are You?
They expect to hear I'm A-OK
When they don't, they don't notice
They just carry on anyway

What's the point to the question
If your answer isn't heard?
But then, I ask the tough ones
And I think this bullshit is absurd

If you ask me my opinion
Don't ignore my reply
It's really irritating
When you don't even try

I'm trying to be truthful
To be honest and transparent
If you get to really know me
That should be readily apparent

Long ago I lost my filters
My last fuck has finally flown
I'm stubborn, blunt and determined
These are traits I honestly own

If you're looking for a frank assessment
I'm the gal for you
Otherwise I suggest you keep on scrolling
But thanks for passing through.

THE POTTER'S WHEEL

In the darkest hours of morning
I sit and search my soul
You know what I've discovered?
It is pretty old

It's had more than one lifetime
This one isn't the first
I've had some that were better
And some that were worse

The wheel spins ever onward
Around and around it goes
Where it will end up stopping
None of us really knows

Each turn around is different
New lessons to be learned
Wisdom is slow in coming
For that is something earned

You sit now upon the potter's wheel
You're the potter and the clay
How will you decide to fashion yourself?
What will you keep and throw away?

This earthly incarnation
Is just another page in your souls' book
It's what you decide to do with it
That makes people stand up and take a look

So knowing that you are the master
Of your own life and fate
Are you going to make something of it,
Or wait until it's too late?

RAGE

I've tried to contain the beast I call Rage
I've built it a solid, sturdy cage

I tried to bury it deep inside
But I've found there's no place it can hide

Rage can creep up on you unexpected
In the moment you're feeling rejected

Rage can make you want to explode
It can be such a heavy load

You can scream and cry and rage for days
Rage makes us all feel half-crazed

I tried to stuff Rage in a box
It would not stay there, it broke the locks

Rage is a fire that does consume
All the happiness that's in a room

Rage is a difficult beast to master
My first attempts were a complete disaster

You cannot run and you cannot hide
You're forced to step up and decide

The first step that you can take
Is a nice deep breath, don't hesitate

As you breathe, count to ten
Take a moment and do it again

Look deep inside to find the source
Heal yourself first, of course

It's a challenging thing to learn to do
Taking charge of the emotions that live within you

But as you learn to order your life and mind
You'll be amazed at the peace there to find

Then one day you'll finally see
You've opened that door and set yourself free.

WORD PLAY

Words, words
Come into my head
It's kind of amazing
Some of the things that I've said

Words, words
I love rhythm and rhyme
I like playing with words
All of the time

Words, words
Go with the flow
So many ways
To put them together you know

Words, words
Watch what you say
You never know when your words
Will come back to haunt you someday

Words, words
Are they truth or lies?
So many hidden meanings
Can be hidden inside

Words, words
Choose them with care
You never know who is listening
Or whom is aware

Words, words
Some old and some new
How you arrange them
Is all up to you

Words, words
Come on and give them a try
If nothing else, playing with them
Helps the time to pass by

Words, words
Was it something I said?
Did I really just say that
Or was it all in my head?

MIRROR TALK

You never look
Before you leap
You appear shallow
When in fact you're deep

You don't walk
When you can run
You never quit
Until the job is done

You're always up
At dawns' first light
You're the last one to bed
Late at night

You like to give
Second chances
At heart you remain
A hopeful romantic

You never say no
When you can say yes
You always search
For the very best

You won't turn back
You just forge ahead
I know you won't stop
Until you're dead.

MEANT TO BE

Gazing into the mirror
What do I see?
Someone else
Staring back at me.

How did she find me?
Where did I go?
Where is the me,
That I used to know?

This person I see here,
Isn't young or old;
She's bold as brass,
Precious as gold.

There may be some lines,
That show on her face;
But she carries them,
With courage and grace.

Her smile may be broken,
Her hair may be thin;
But this doesn't dim the light,
That shines from within.

If you look in the mirror
And all that you see,
Is the meat suit you wear
In this reality,

You're missing the concept
That we exist eternally;
The limitless potential
We are meant to be.

SEWN TIGHT

I took my disappointments, my setbacks,
My broken dreams
I threw them into a bag
And sewed tight the seams

I'm brewing an elixir
Of life's experiences instead
If you drink it it's intoxicating
It goes straight to your head

To me it doesn't matter
If you're the one on top
Just keep moving forward
And choose not to stop

Life is an alchemical process
To experience it is divine
You'll find it gets sweeter
The longer it ripens on the vine

So now I'm going to sit back and enjoy it
Sip by slow sip
Only the finest vintage
For this one of a kind life trip.

NEW PATH

It felt like I was drowning
In an ocean of my tears
Where I cried away my hopes
And faced all my fears

For a long time
I was able to float
Then life came along
And swamped my boat

No matter how fast
How furiously I bailed
I didn't go under
But I still felt I'd failed

It took me awhile
To rest and recover
I lost the old way
Then I discovered another

I'm still not certain
Where this new path will lead
I'm grateful my feet have found it
And I walk on confidently indeed

Step by step
Breath by breath
I can pause if I need too
At my own request

One more time
My dreams set sail
As I slide off into the horizon
Past the veil.

WHAT WILL IT TAKE

I'm crying bitter
Hot, scalding tears
While I sit here and confront
All of my doubts and my fears

I'm reviewing my successes and failures
From over the years
There's been twists and turns
The path hasn't always been clear

I'm sitting here wondering
What did I do right?
Was it all worth it,
The struggle and fight?

What have I lost?
What have I gained?
What things are different?
What's stayed the same?

I feel like I'm stuck running
On a great big hamster wheel
I run furiously around
But keep ending up here

What will it take
To finally see change?
I don't really know,
But I'm tired of this game.

MONEY'S WORTH

I sat and gazed into the mirror today
There are lines on my face that won't go away
Little, tiny, finely etched lines
Their presence reminds me of the passage of time

Sometimes I wonder, where it all went
Where did it go, this time that I've spent?
I was a spendthrift with it once, you know
But I've learned the beauty of, "go with the flow"

All that's left is memories
And I keep those close to me
Precious people and things that I see
Allowing me to grow and be free

Every moment transcended time
They are forever imprinted, engraved in my mind
I also discovered the white in my hair
Wondering, "when the hell did that get there?"

In the morning when I wake
Oh my gosh my joints they ache
Reminding me, what's the use
Of all those years of bodily abuse

I rise and stretch and moan and groan
Thanking God I'm all alone
I stretch, move and dance you see
Until things move more easily

I know that people watch and laugh
Who gives a shit, I have a blast!
Dancing now across the floor
Open up the bathroom door

Start the water, get it hot
Get in the shower; that hits the spot!
I'm just preparing to start my day
I really know no other way

Some days I need to take it slow
Others, I just jump up and go
I've found being patient with myself
Is so much better for my health

Now I rise and great the sun
And I also gaze upon it when the day is done
I have changed to embrace my life
According to my own advice

In that knowledge I've finally found
A reason I want to hang around
For a few more years here on this earth
'Cause man, I want my money's worth!

SOME DAYS

Some days I'm high
Some days I'm low
Some days I feel
Like I have a long way to go

Some days I laugh
Some days I cry
Some days I ponder
All of the reasons why

Why must we argue?
Why must we fight?
Why are there so many definitions
Of what's wrong and what's right?

Why can't we wake up
And realize it's time to stand up
To do what's right
Time to make a choice, fight your own fight

If you want to see change
It's all up to you
No one else
Can do what you do

You make a difference
Each and every day
It's up to you to decide
The role that you'll play

Do you want to be thrust
Out upon center stage?
Or is being a part of the chorus
What keeps you engaged?

Set your mind free
Break out of your box
Give something new a chance
You may discover it rocks

Some days I jump
To make that unknown leap
Some days I fail
And I land in a heap

But every day I wake up
And I keep giving it a try
Because at the end of the day
I'm the reason I fly.

UNDERSTANDING

How do I explain
The way I'm feeling inside
I want you to know
And God knows I've tried

My thoughts are all scrambled
And tied up in a knot
I try to follow the storyline
But I keep losing the plot

My insides are twisted
My head is spinning
It feels like I'm losing
Even when I am winning

I know that you can't see
What goes on in my head
I still keep on smiling
When I want to scream instead

I wish you could understand
And relate to this pain
Then I wouldn't feel so lost and confused
And so filled with shame

I'm doing my best
Just to get through today
Until I can lay down to sleep
And try to dream it all away

Maybe, now
You might have a clue
And imagine how this would feel
If it was you.

NIGHTTIME VISITORS

Wrestling with my demons
All alone in the dark
I feel like I'm swimming in water
Surrounded by sharks

It they reach out and catch me
I fear that I'll drown
I'm struggling to stay afloat
While I slowly sink down

If I can hold on
Just get through the night
I know things will look different
In mornings first light

In the meantime I sit
I hope and I pray
That my courage holds steady
And I can keep them at bay.

COSMIC DICE

Love and hate
Heaven and hell
Two sides of a coin
That I know well

Sometimes it feels
Like it all hangs on a toss
Sometimes the path
Makes me feel like I'm lost

A cosmic dice game
Or is there a choice?
Do we make our own fate
As we find our voice?

I have found life
To be sharp and dual edged
It doesn't work out
When you hedge your bets

To look and to leap
Has just been my way
But no matter the experience
I'm still here today.

HAVE TO CONSIDER

Some days I get tired
For this road is very long
Sometimes I get weary
Of trying to sing the same old song.

Some days I have trouble
Seeing the forest for the trees
Sometimes the problems I uncover
Bring me to my knees

Some days the losses
Seem like they outnumber the gains
Sometimes it's hard to move
Without screaming from the pain

Some days I look and wonder
Am I doing anything right
Sometimes I just want peace
Because I'm tired of the fight

Some days all of this bullshit
Really wears me down
Sometimes I force a smile
When all I want to do is frown

Some days I'll admit my perspective
Is a bit askew
Sometimes I have to consider
Perhaps I need to change my point of view.

VAST OCEAN

It seems that I've cried great oceans of tears
Clinging to hope but drowning in fears

You know it can be so draining this fight
Climbing up out of the darkness and into the light

Searching around for something to grasp
Unable to recognize a chance until it's passed

In this vast ocean we feel so alone
Not realizing millions of other drops also call this home

We are but a droplet caught up in this tide
Tossed and turned and swept along for the ride

One day that current pushed me towards shore
Opening new vistas for me to explore

Brilliant new things for me to do and discover
As day by day I began to recover

But once I began to truly open my heart
That's when I knew it was a new start.

CHILD OF MY HEART

Child of my heart
Living expression of love
May blessings rain down upon you
From the good Lord above

I wish for you
Every good thing
The joy and happiness
That this life may bring

I always want to see
That smile on your face
While I hold you gently
In my loving embrace

Oh little girl
Who lives in my heart
Learning those lessons
Was such a fabulous start

Now that you've learned
That there is a whole new way
I'm so proud of you
For what you've had to say

It's amazing to see
What you've overcome
I'm constantly amazed
At what you have done

The hardest thing
I had to learn to do
Was to simply open my heart
And share this with you.

YOU CAN'T

You can't rise up
If you keep letting yourself down
You can't learn to fly
With your feet on the ground

You can't open new doors
When your mind stays closed
You can't mind the thorns
If you wish to pluck the rose

You can't scream
And make no sound
You can't stay lost
When you've been found

You can't make friends
With someone you hate
You can't get started early
When you arrive late

You can't dive deep
Into a shallow pool
You can't act like an idiot
And have people think you're cool

You can't leave
If you stay
You can't ever find tomorrow
It's always a day away.

CRAZY OR INSANE

Am I crazy
Or am I insane
Some say they're different
I think they're the same

It's a fine line
On a steep, slippery slope
When it feels like your brain is sliding
As you struggle to cope

Still you cast an illusion
You say that you're fine
When deep down inside
You stand toeing the line

Just one more time now
Into that dark abyss
As you think to yourself
I'm so fucking tired of this

Crazy or insane
It's such an illusory game
It doesn't matter if you win or you lose
In the end the results are the same.

MUD

I have mud on my fingers
I have mud between my toes
You don't want to know
The places this mud goes

Mud from the river
Mud from the yard
The four inches of mud
Make this job so fucking hard

The mud sucks you in
The mud drags you down
The mud is everywhere
There's plenty to go around

People are slinging mud at each other
Up, down, left and right
Why is it in the middle of this disaster
All they can do is loot and fight?

I have mud on my skin
Mud in my hair
I'm so tired of drowning in the mud
That is fucking everywhere.

ONE MORE TIME

Is it the end
Or a new beginning?
You lost it all
But still you're winning

Isn't it darkest
Before the dawn?
You still have your memories
And they linger on.

Your courage doesn't hang
Like a fragile thread
You keep moving forward
In spite of the dread

You're wading through
Such chaos and destruction
This unprecedented event
Needs no more introduction

Step by step
You walk your path
Knowing these times
They won't last

So it's one more time
Into the abyss
And perhaps someday
I can forget about this.

LEARNING THE WORD

You say I'm too sensitive
I wear my heart on my sleeve
You say I'm difficult
And not easy to please

You say I'm picky
I'm a pain in the ass
You say I need to slow down
I'm moving too fast

You say I'm a zebra
I don't blend into the herd
You say I am one of kind
I have a talent for the written word

You say I learn the hard way
I tend to crash and burn
But I think the most important thing
Is that I do, indeed, learn.

DEVIL'S DANCE

I've danced with the devil
A passionate tango in the rain
It was twisted and complicated
And I'm tempted, once again

It's such an enticement
That experience we shared
I believed that he loved me
I believed that he cared

So many things
That he offered to me
But everything has its price
Nothing is for free

It starts so slowly
It's so expertly played
You don't notice you've been taken
Until you're lost in the maze

The twists and the turns
Become too much for you
You wonder to yourself
When will this be through?

But even when it ends
You can't help but crave
All of those things
That made you his slave

So you sit and you wonder
Night after night
Give up and give in
Or keep up the good fight?

NO ONE

No one knows
What you're feeling inside
No one knows
What you're able to hide

No one knows
Just how high your highs
No one knows
Just how low your lows

No one knows
Your hopes and dreams
No one knows
How you cry and scream

No one knows
You feel so alone
No one knows
You have an empty home

No one knows
The lengths you'll go
No one knows
That you're taking it slow

No one knows
Or can feel your pain
No one knows
That you're going insane

No one knows
No one cares
No one knows
They are unaware

No one knows
No one knows
That's how it goes
No one knows.

A WAR

You say you talk to angels
Spirits, demons and guides
I think you have a war
Going on inside

Who am I to say
What you do or do not see
Just because I don't experience it
Doesn't mean it's not your reality

It sounds really busy
All the chatter inside your mind
I can understand how your sanity
Would fray and unwind

Are the voices divine
Or do they mean you are insane?
No matter whom I ask,
The answers are never the same.

FORGIVE

I'M LEARNING

I'm learning the secrets
You hold in your heart
The ones you've kept hidden
And chose to never impart

I'm learning of your past
Of all you endured
I'm learning of your strength
Your voice, it is heard

I'm learning of your troubles
Your worries and doubts
It's about time you decided
To let all of those out

I'm learning of your joys
Your hopes and your dreams
I'm getting to know you again
And I like what I'm seeing

I'm learning that brief moments in time
Are just not enough
And that deep down inside
You're not really that tough

I'm learning that in this lifetime
I can't call you mine
And the relationship we have
Is hard to define

I'm learning that once again
We are both rediscovering the way
And I hope once we find it
We'll be able to stay.

BRINGING TROUBLE HOME

I smile and laugh
Despite my anger and fear
It's a little coping mechanism I've developed
To help me get through the years

I brush forward my hair
To cover my tears
I cover my ears
And try not to hear

All those terrible things
Said with a laugh and a jeer
Some days you don't know
How hard it is being here

Yet you always say,
Run along my dear,
Company is coming
No, they're here.

IN THE MEANTIME

I don't know why you expect to find
The person that you thought you knew
You've been gone so many years,
In the meantime, deep inside I grew

I'm not the person that you left
Or the one you used to know
I have taken every opportunity
For me to learn and grow

Perhaps we can explore each other
In a way we never have before
But unless you lose your assumptions
You can keep walking right out that door

You haven't stood beside me
On this life journey that I took
My whole life isn't open to you
You can't read it in a book

Your mind can fill in the blanks
The filled the time that I have spent
But until you ask and listen
You'll only guess at where that time went

You cannot force the present
To return to what has passed
When you finally understand this
Then we might have a chance

I've taken accountability
For all of my mistakes
I can't get by just claiming
That it's all in the hands of fate

If you'd like to join me
There's something you need to do
Wake up and finally listen
And make some changes too.

THE MIRROR

What do you see
When you look in the mirror?
Is it your best self,
Or is it your worst fear?

What thoughts fill your head
In the darkness of night?
Do you sing in your dreams,
Or cry out in fright?

What words leave your lips
Each and every day?
Are you generous and kind
Or do you push others away?

What emotions exist
In the depths of your heart?
Does love hold you together
Or hate tear you apart?

SAID UNSAID

I wish you could go back through time
Then maybe you could understand
All those experiences that shaped me
That helped make me who I am

You have such a hard time believing
Things that you cannot see
You don't believe what I've told you
Is how things used to be

You've drawn your own conclusions
Which have nothing to do with facts
You don't remember saying the words
But I wish you could take them back

I learned about expectations and obligations
It never felt like love
Nothing was ever good enough
When push came right down to shove

You've express your disappointment and judgement
You've never held it back
Yet you wonder why I run away
When you're back on the attack

It doesn't matter what I say and do
It's never been enough
Whenever I expressed how hard things were
What I heard was "toughen up"

So who is it that you should blame
When I turn and walk away?
For years I wanted to talk about it
Always being told, not today

So the cycle keeps continuing
This emotional roller coaster
The peaks and valleys haven't evened out
Even though I'm growing older

All I can do is get off this train
Before it barrels down the tracks
I don't want to say anything more
Because the words can't be taken back.

I RELEASE YOU

I release you, I release you
I set you free
I free myself from this attachment
That binds you to me

I release you, I release you
I open wide the door
You already walked through there
For you live here no more

I release you, I release you
Good luck and good bye
I'm grateful to have loved you
But I can no longer cry

I release you, I release you
I reclaim my own light
May it continue to burn
Clearly and bright

I release you, I release you
I wish you the best
This chapter has ended
Now I lay it to rest.

OF THE GAME

You're trying to run from a fate
That you cannot escape
By the time you realized it
It was already too late

You had no warning
Of the twists and the turns
That they would keep on repeating
Until the lesson's been learned

You keep spinning around
Like a line on a broken reel
The endless circle
Has long since lost its appeal

You know that's there's only one way
For you to exit this ride
A veil and a barrier
That remains there to divide

You've tried to punch your own ticket
For it's your own grand design
Yet you keep waking up each morning
Time after time

You look around and you wonder
Why nothing makes sense
You're tired of the manipulation
Senseless greed and violence

One more day you have
You wonder what's it all for
As you get dressed and get going
Then you head out the door

You work and you play
You spend and you save
You live your best life
But still end up in a grave

Living and dying
It's all part of the game
For now matter how often we repeat it
The results are the same

So what chance will you take
Right now while you live
Will you try everything once
And experience all life has to give

Or will you sit and lament
At the end of you days
All you could have done
And what you let slip away?

CHILDHOOD WISHES

I wish I had
Something more to say
I wish you weren't
Going away

I wish I could
Play all day
I wish it wouldn't
Rain today

I wish I may
I wish I might
I pray that I
Can get it right

I wish I was
Thin and tall
I wish I could
Win them all

I wish I could
Stay awake all night
I wish that people
Wouldn't argue and fight

I wish I was
Writing a song
I wish you all would
Sing along

I wish you wouldn't
Walk away
I wish we had
Just one more day

I wish my wishes
Could save the day
But you grow up and learn
It's just not that way.

NO SHARING, NO CARING

No one knows
If you're high or low
If you got there quickly
Or moved real slow

No one shares
Your hopes and dreams
No one hears
Your silent screams

No one cares
Of your fate
But you should
Before it's too late

No one helped you up
No one dragged you down
Time to step up
And adjust your crown

If no one listens
Because you don't share
How can you blame them
When they're unaware?

REMEMBER WHEN

I can remember
Who you were then
For I like to play
At remember when

I'm not certain
When you changed
But you no longer
Are the same

I miss the person
I used to know
I have to wonder now
Where did he go?

What has happened
In your life?
What were the joys
The pain, the strife?

What were the challenges
That you found?
What were the things
That turned you around?

I'll always wonder
About the time that's passed
And what was truly
Meant to last.

WHAT WILL YOU SEE?

Did you ever look
At that person in the mirror
And wonder how in the hell
Did I end up here?

Have you ever lain down
To sleep at night
And just tossed and turned
Until mornings first light?

Do your days sometime blend
One right into the other
Do you ever wonder
What else there is for you to discover?

Have you ever gotten up
And just gone away?
Just hitting the road
No place to go, no where to stay?

Do you sit and wonder
Where the time went?
Do you ponder your experiences
And what they all meant?

Have you finally discovered
What lifts you up?
What fills your heart
Like an overflowing cup?

Do you wonder
What to say and what to do
Why nothing good
Ever seems to happen to you?

Have you ever looked
Deep into your heart?
Don't you think
It's about time you start?

What will you see
When you journey within
When you quiet the voices
And silence the din?

PHOENIX

The Phoenix was eerily silent
Even as she fell
For even as she plummeted to earth
She'd already been through hell

She'd been down that path before
And she knew it well
But where she'd end up
Only time would tell

No one expected
That she would fall
For they were all surprised
She'd ever risen at all

She was puzzled by the way
They took delight in her pain
The way they seemed to feed
Upon her guilt and shame

Even though she'd resisted
And fought her way back into the light
She was tired and weary
She was sick of the fight

Somehow she knew
She needed to lay her burden down
Or this time when she sunk
She would do nothing but drown.

HEAVEN SENT

I feel like my soul
Is a little confused
For it's been battered and beaten
And a little abused

You may not think
That my story is true
But what do you know?
It didn't happen to you.

You may believe
My life's heaven sent
But I can assure you
That's not how it went

Nothing came easy
It's always a fight
But still I keep trying
To do what is right

Unless you've walked
A few miles in my shoes
It my be difficult to understand
My point of view

So while you sit there
With your judgment and blame
Perhaps you should try living it
And see if your results are the same.

INNER GRACE

Suddenly I looked around
I couldn't believe what I had found

This amazing mirror appeared in space
I gazed within and beheld my face

But it was the strangest thing you see
For what I beheld was two, of me!

They say that opposites attract
This is true for myself in fact

As I peered at who was revealed there
Suddenly I became aware

This was the other half of me
The side that most don't get to see

I found that I had hidden her well
How long ago I could not tell

At first she was a little shy
I knew that I just had to try

To draw her out of that fragile shell
I felt my heart began to swell

It hurt my chest it opened so wide
As we reunited deep inside

A joyous reunion we did share
Learning each other with gentle care

An amazing moment of inner grace
And the smile still remains upon my face.

NOT UNEXPECTED

Disappointed
But not unexpected,
Your emotional withdrawal
Left me feeling quite dejected

Once I took a minute
To really think things through
I realized that this is a continuation
Of an endless game with you

For many years I walked that razor edge
Unable to stop even while I bled
I always kept coming back for more
Never guessing you were keeping score.

I finally refused to walk your maze
No longer do I feel half-crazed
It was time for me to let you go
It wasn't very easy though

I struggled when I felt the loss
Of the place you filled despite the cost
Funny how I could miss the pain
The guilt, the blame and the shame.

Day by day I seek and find
Peace and calm within my mind
This lesson I learned once again
Of the qualities of those I would call friend.

HEAL

EMPTY PROMISES

I don't want your empty promises
Wrapped up with a pretty little bow
You repackaged yourself for your purposes
The glitter was all for show

You really were quite clever
Adept at the game you played
I tried to navigate your deadly maze
I ended up getting flayed

Still you just can't understand
Why I won't participate
I did for so many years
For I learned the rules quite late

There is no way to win this game
For no matter which hand you choose
The can only be one clear winner
And everyone else does lose

So I choose not to ante up to the table
To play a rigged game with losing hands
I pushed my chair back and walked away
Using all the strength at my command

I certainly wasn't easy
In fact, it's been quite hard
The wound may just be healing
But it'll still leave a scar.

ALL TIME

I want you to know
I wish you were here
I wish your arms
Were holding me near

I wish you were beside me
In the middle of the night
So you could gather me close
When I call out in fright

I want to wake up
And see your face
To begin and end each day
Simply; in your embrace

I wish that one day
I can just call you mine
And someday that one day
Will last for all time.

BATTERED

I'll never forget
How you made me feel so confused
How you tried to convince me
That your actions weren't abuse

I'll never forget
Your whispered lies and threats
How you continually reminded me
It wasn't over just yet

I'll never forget
The look of enjoyment in your eyes
And the satisfaction you got
From hearing my cries

I'll never forget
Those words that you said
How you cut out my heart
Then stood and watched while I bled

I'll never forget
Lying there on the floor
In a pool of my own blood
As you walked out the door

I'll never forget
I'm not sure I'll forgive
But finally without you
I've begun to live.

THE WIND WHISPERS

The wind speaks in whispers
as it blows through the trees
Brushing the grass back and forth
as it catches the breeze

Snowy white laundry
dances outside on the line
Moving in ways
I find hard to define

The warmth of the sun
kisses my skin
I stop for a moment
and drink it all in

The scent in the air
is heady and fine
The only way I can describe it
is truly sublime

The gardens lie empty
for the harvest has passed
The cupboards are full
and bulging at last

In this abundance
we take time to rejoice
We fill up our glasses
and lift up our voice

We gather together to celebrate
another turn of the wheel
As we work together
to prepare this fine meal

Take some time
to enjoy your repast
Savor those moments
and stretch them to last

Time is always well spent
with family and friends
Let it live on in your memory
where those moments never end

Open the door
and go for a walk
Let dinner settle
and take time to talk

Listen to the wind whisper
its soft accompaniment
Smile in contentment
knowing your time's been well spent.

SUN CLIMB

When I wake early in the morning
Before I rise from my bed
I take a minute to set my intention
And put positive thoughts in my head

The room is dark and still
All my neighbors are asleep
I so love this time of day
Into my soul the peace does seep

The early morning silence
Begins to be broken by some sounds
The waking of the birds
Is heralded by their songs which abound

I watch the sun climb the horizon
As I start my day
I breathe and stretch and meditate
Letting all my stress drift away

It's a great way to get grounded
And to begin my day
You might want to try it
Life's so much better this way.

OLD PARADIGM

I never knew the unknown
Could be so fair
I took the path less traveled,
And I ended up there.

In order to journey
You must first make a start
Begin by opening your mind,
Then follow with your heart.

Inside you will find
All the answers you seek
Despite what you're thinking,
This makes you strong, not weak.

It took years
To end up in this bind
It will take more time
To begin to unwind

The tangles and twists
Are an integral part of this weave
That until recently
We were unable to perceive.

Patiently we must learn
To retrace the thread
Back to the places
We would rather not tread.

But once you've opened up
The way for this change
It's amazing to discover
How your life is rearranged.

What was once so important
That falls away,
Your perspective shifts
To a whole new way.

In your heart
You learn to embrace
The love and the light
The joy and the grace.

Shifting your focus
Makes you much more aware
Of all that can be found
When you venture out there.

So take the time
Make that start
Open your mind
And open your heart

For you too
Shall play your part
If from this old paradigm
We wish to depart!

SHADOWS AND VOICES

Sometimes I see people inside of my head
Some are the living, others are dead

They don't always show up when I call
I'm fact some days they don't appear at all

So many voices begging to be heard
To whisper of secrets they have endured

Shadows and voices in the night
When the darkness eclipses the light

See the stars light the sky
They are the reaches to which I may fly

Music of the flute and drum
The only sound I make is AUM

Then in the endless vistas in my mind
Many pathways do unwind

Twist and turn as you walk the path
Fading through the blades of grass

Here the trees are evergreen
Though it remains to common eyes unseen

Approach the gates and inquire within
Tell me now, did they let you in?

INNER VISTA

Have you rediscovered
that joy that you'd lost?
Have you scaled those mountains
you never thought you could cross?

Have you opened your heart
as well as your mind?
If you have,
what did you find?

It's pretty amazing
when you can look and see
Things from a different perspective
or three

There are no limits
within your mind
Lose your expectations
leave them far behind

This inner vista
of which you are now aware
many mysteries and clues
we find unfolding there

Dynamic and changing
and always in flux
We become aware of the multiple dimensions
Existing within us

Once we discover
this magical place
It's then
we can begin to embrace

Reverence for all these things
that I can see
The myriad of lives
that are interconnected within me

From the rocks and the grass
and the leafy green trees
The animals and fish
and birds and the bees

It's amazing to feel
this universal embrace
When we learn to see life
from our sacred heart space

I offer this to you
as a new point of view
As you've been struggling
to try to see things through

Now that the intentions
of the collective are heard
It's time now to gather
and then spread the word.

THE NEW ELEVATION

There are some who believe
They can learn how to fly
And others who wonder
Why even try?

But if you give up
Before you've even begun
Nothing new
Would ever get done.

You cannot soar
Unless you first test your wings
And adjust to the changes
The new elevation brings

Those who say they can't
Shouldn't stand in the way of those who are
It's those who can overcome and adapt
Who will soar amongst the stars.

A SEA OF SACRED SOULS

Some days I feel like I'm afloat
On the USS Universal Life Boat
I see these souls flailing around
I reach out and try to grab them before they drown

There are many hands aboard this ship
Navigating this complex human life trip
It's tough to sail the course with ease
When one wrong tack brings you to your knees

Suddenly at the moment when you shout
You see this hand reaching out
The compass swings round and turns about
Now there is no room for you to doubt

You're awash in a sea of synchronicity
Putting you exactly where we need to be
For you think I am rescuing you,
When I'm actually saving me.

RADIANT TOUCH

I was sleeping there in the darkness of my room
When suddenly I was awakened by the call of the moon

My house began to fill with a radiant light
I began to see shadows in the night

I looked up and suddenly on my face
Your radiant touch filled me with grace

I sat in wonder and then I cried
Unable to contain this joy inside

I had to get outside to sing and dance
Knowing nothing is just circumstance

A beautiful blessing to end my day
And I wouldn't have it any other way.

IN THE CENTER

Seeking center in the silence
Blocking out the waves of violence
Reaching deep, down within
Quiet the voices, calm the din

In the city I feel the pain
The angst of many is such a drain
In my solitude I can recover
Grounding with Gaia, my earthly mother

Trapped in a metal and cement cage
All I feel is others rage
So many angry, alone and scared
Lost souls, everywhere

But once I feel the blades of grass
I know that I am home at last
I simply sit and look around
At nature's beauty I have found

I take a breath and breathe it in
Feel that calmness as it begins
Another breath and I wash away
The chaos that has come my way

I lie back and watch the sky
Lost in the clouds drifting by
The energy of the sun warms my skin
I drink it down and draw it in

As I became a channel for the light
I know I'm doing something right
In this bliss I'd love to stay
It's a much better way

Take that love and spread it round
Try to spread that joy I've found
For when your heart has grown so much within
You have no choice but to let love in.

RUNNING

If I were to share with you
The secrets of my heart
Would you stay and listen
Or push us farther apart?

Would you gather me close
At the end of the day
Hold me tight in your arms
Until the fear went away?

When I awake screaming
In the middle of the night
Would you comfort me then
Or draw back in fright?

I'm not really certain
If you truly know me
If you wish to learn
The many things I can be

This journey is uncertain
Some days we struggle and fight
It can be so very hard
Those days and those nights

We're trying so hard
To understand
This connection we share
Makes its own demands

I cannot escape
This feeling inside
From the thoughts and the feelings
There is no where to hide

All of this churning
As we try to avoid
Emotional overwhelm
Becoming lost in the void

Bringing out
Into the light
The fears and insecurities
That plague us at night

Confronting them all
One by one
Is part of the healing
It must be done

Sharing the burden
Lessens it you see
So I hope that you
Can share yours with me

There is no escape
From what lives in your mind
You must confront it
You know that it's time

I remain here
Quiet and true
Just trying to share
Me with you

Patiently I wait
For you to decide
Are you running again
Or along for the ride?

UNEASE BEHIND DISEASE

Depression is when
You sleep all day
Because none of your problems
Will go away

Insomnia is where
You lay awake all night
Tossing and turning
Until mornings first light

Grief is when
You're world's so small
No one else
Seems to matter at all

Anxiety is when
Your mind keep racing
As you dread
What you are facing

Anorexia is when
You starve yourself thin
Because you feel
Dead within

Obsession-compulsion is when
You count, count, count
No matter how many times you wipe that spot
You can't get it out

Cutting is when
You feel so numb
You only feel something
When you see your blood run

Addiction is when
You feed the hungry ghost inside
Searching for things
You've been denied

PTSD is when
You keep flashing back
To that moment of
Your physical or mental attack

Schizophrenia is when
Many strange voices
Overwhelm your life
And leave you no choices

Munchausen by proxy is when
Someone is hurting you
To get the attention
They feel they're entitled to

Codependency is when
You can't bear to be apart
Even knowing it's all wrong
Right from the start

Gaslighting is when
Someone is telling you
It's just not that bad
Those things you've gone through

Healing is when
You acknowledge your pain
When you stop focusing on the loses
And celebrate each gain

Growth is when
You learn what's triggering you
And you take the time
To work those issues through

Recovery is when
You've moved past what has been
And begin remembering fondly
Do you remember when?

UNIVERSAL WINDS

Winds of change, blow through me
Lift my spirit and set me free
Take me higher so I may roam
Throughout this Universe we call home

Winds of change blow through my chimes
The music calls me, it's sublime
So many vistas I do see
Reaching out to welcome me

Many are places I've seen before
They exist just outside my open door
Some are future, some are past
Amazing how they blend at last

Backwards and forwards, weave through time
The divine pattern is so sublime
Drifting freely in this place
Out of time, out of space

I lift my face to the rising sun
Another new day has begun
The winds of change now blow me home
From the many places my spirit roamed.

MOVING ON

Here I sit
Amidst the debris
Sorting through left behind
Pieces of me

Bits and pieces
I can place in a box
But that's isn't the repository
For the rest of my thoughts

I came to a place
I never thought I would be
Now I'm rediscovering what it means
To finally be free

One more time
To walk across the floor
One last time
To close and lock the door.

A BETTER WAY

Here I sit
alone at last
Pondering all
that has come to pass

This life has been
so many things
Predictable is not one of them
Or so it seems

I've wandered far
Across this land
And tried so hard
To understand

Just what it is
That changes fate
And turns people
Toward rage and hate

Something
Must have changed you see
For this is not
how it was meant to be

We were all
Born in love
Sent here
From the Lord above

But clearly something
did go wrong
For so many failed
to learn the song

To be heart centered
in peace and love
And in so doing
rise above

Those of us
who have found that space
Are working to make this world
a better place

If that is also
your point of view
I'd love it
if you would join us too

We can join
in our collected stance
Gather together
and take a chance

Time to show
the world a better way
Ensuring that
it's here to stay.

LA BELLA LUNA

La Bella Luna, you're a beautiful sight
I bathe in your energy by my fire tonight

Here between the earth and sky
I stretch my arms way up high

I feel your light upon my face
As you bless me with your grace

La Bella Luna, I welcome thee
I'm a child of your light and you set me free

Here beneath the moon and stars
I know that I can wonder far

I can feel your heavenly pull
Through this connection my heart is full

La Bella Luna, as you grace the sky
Hear my plea, hear my cry

Open the veil and part the way
So cosmic forces come into play

Fill my heart with love and light
As I keep watch with you through the night.

PUZZLE ME

I've realized,
You are not my puzzle to solve
I don't have the keys to release you
From your self imposed prison
Trapped by your own expectations
Useless longings for yesterday
For time is transient

I've realized,
That I've been viewing life
Through a distorted lens
Never noticing the smoke
So subtle clouding my perceptions
But the wind of change
Has parted that almost imperceptible veil

I've realized,
That I've begun to see things clearly
For myself
Colored by my own experiences
The wisdom I've earned
Such as it is
And in so doing

I've realized,
I'm beginning to recover
Those scattered pieces of myself
Assembling them into a beautiful mosaic
Fragile fractals joined with gold
For I was always my own puzzle to solve.

ABOUT LESLIE

Retired from a twenty-five-year career as an emergency, critical care and flight nurse, Leslie has been sharing her poetic vision with tens of thousands of social media followers since 2018.

She currently lives, writes and finds peace and inspiration in the foothills of the Blue Ridge Mountains.

Follow her on Facebook and Instagram @paradoxicalphoenix.

https://www.paradoxicalphoenix.com

www.ingramcontent.com/pod-product-compliance
Lightning Source LLC
Chambersburg PA
CBHW021504090426
42739CB00007B/453